MUTTS of the MASTERS

By Michael Patrick

MJF BOOKS

NEW YORK

Published by MJF Books
Fine Communications
Two Lincoln Square
60 West 66th Street
New York, NY 10023

Mutts of the Masters
ISBN 1-56731-336-1

Copyright © 1996 by Pat Welch and Mike Dowdall
Additional illustration by Sandy Reznor, Tom Soltesz, and Al Stutrud

This edition published by arrangement with Andrews McMeel Publishing.

Printed in Singapore
MJF Books and the MJF colophon are trademarks of Fine Creative Media, Inc.

10   9   8   7   6   5   4   3   2   1

MUTTS of the
MASTERS

INTRODUCTION

MUTTS OF THE MASTERS

Dogs – one has only to look around – are everywhere. There are dogs at the laundromat, dogs at the library, dogs in parks and city streets, dogs at football games and supermarkets, at PTA meetings and barbecues, at political rallies and parades. It follows that there are also dogs in artists' studios – and always have been. That these dogs should show up in the work produced in such ateliers is not merely natural; it is inevitable. And yet the dog, so often an embarrassment to himself and others, so regularly in need of containment or even banishment, has commonly been expunged from the products of the artists with whom this book is concerned – which is to say, every artist from Michelangelo to Matisse. So here they are: the dogs who were sent away (or painted over), but who somehow always re-emerge, as innocent, oblivious, and embarrassing as ever.

Frustrated by the art-buying public's resistance to the Impressionist movement, Paul Cezanne decided to produce a series of paintings which he felt could not fail to appeal to a more general audience. This one, *Dogs Playing Poker*, was the first of four, including *Dogs Drinking Absinthe*, *Dogs Regarding a Bust of Napoleon*, and *Dogs Disrupting a Lawn Party*. The series was introduced at Le Galerie Toujours in Paris in the fall of 1889, and was the most resounding failure of his career. Though the public was unanimous in its rejection, critics were divided: most declared that only a fool could believe people would ever buy pictures of dogs playing cards; a few maintained that Cezanne was simply ahead of his time.

Through history, the art world has experienced many fleeting fads and fashions. One of the most whimsical – yet shortest-lived – occurred in England in the 1500s, when it was the rage to have one's portrait painted in the form of whatever animal the artist imagined one most resembled. Ladies-in-waiting became does or unicorns, noted lords were portrayed as warhorses or rams, and so on. One enterprising painter took it upon himself to interpret his beloved king and must have had hopes of glory when he presented his canvas at court. Strangely, however, history makes no further mention of the artist – except for the coincidence of someone with the same name being beheaded in the Tower of London the following week – and even more curiously, the entire population seems to have lost interest in their harmless diversion within days.

The enormous undertaking of the Sistine Chapel ceiling required Michelangelo to spend many solitary months at a time, so he acquired Jupiter, a French Porcelaine, to keep him company. Eventually, however, Jupiter became equally bored by the endless hours in an empty room and (as is common with bored dogs) took to chewing whatever he could find. When he found Pope Julius's dressing chamber and destroyed three brand-new pairs of the Shoes of the Fisherman, the enraged pontiff banished Jupiter from the premises. Michelangelo, already chafing under His Holiness's constant tyranny, painted this sarcastic version of the incident on an unfinished panel of the ceiling. The Pope, of course, simply made him paint it over, but Michelangelo later said, "It was worth it. At least that was one time I didn't just take the papal bull."

To test his theory of pointillism, Seurat needed a scene containing many contrasting hues and values, and he chose Paris's *La Grande Jatte* on a typical Sunday afternoon. After months of painstaking work, the huge canvas was shown at a preview gallery opening where it was seen by, among others, a certain M. Printemps, the Second Senior Magistrate of Municipal Parks. M. Printemps was outraged – not at the avant-garde technique but at the number of dogs cavorting in the public areas under his jurisdiction. He immediately instigated emergency legislation, and within days a Certificate of Cease and Desist was delivered to Seurat, whose painting now clearly depicted an unlawful situation, a fact which had been brought to the attention of M. Claude du Vrie, the Second Undersecretary of Public Morals (and M. Printemps's cousin). Anyone who has any experience of French bureaucracy will understand why, in the end, Seurat paid his fine, repainted his picture, and sold his dog.

In his later years, Matisse became increasingly impatient with critics and patrons alike, whom he called "Philistines completely lacking in judgment or taste...who would rather have a picture of their dog done by a housepainter than...art." This image, in cut paper and tempera, is entitled *Canine Dream*, or *What the Dog Does Just Before He Licks Your Face.*

In an effort to be more productive, van Gogh asked his landlady at Arles to provide him with a wake-up call each morning at six. Predictably (the bitter old lady was known far and wide as *La Scourge*), she merely snorted and said, "Get a rooster." (*Prenez un coq.*) Unable to afford either bird or clock, he adopted a local stray dog who kept regular hours, and by sleeping with a biscuit or two under his pillow he was assured of being up with the dawn. Unfortunately, this mutually beneficial arrangement came to an end when *La Scourge*, citing double occupancy, demanded twice the rent.

It was a passing fashion among the idle rich in nineteenth-century Europe to have one's pet's portrait painted by the leading artists of the day. In 1884, though Auguste Renoir was by no means a leading artist and his few patrons were not rich, his wife's sister (whose husband was a moderately prosperous merchant) offered him a commission to paint her Airedale, Oscar. Renoir, who hated (a) portraiture, (b) dogs, and (c) his sister-in-law, refused flatly, saying, *"Jamais de ma vie, mon petit chou fleur,"* which we may translate roughly as "I'd rather drink muddy water and sleep in a hollow log." Mme. Renoir, though more or less neutral on (a) dogs and (b) her sister, had an abiding affection for income-producing commissions. Her only comment was, *"Bouge ton cul, mon petit lapin,"* or, approximately, "Just pick up the brush, Gus."

In 1919, Piet Mondrian was an unknown, unsold, and decidedly unsolvent artist living in a freezing garret in Greenwich Village. Desperate for recognition and groceries, he entered a contest sponsored by a local dog club offering a $50 first prize for the best dog painting. Unaccustomed to drawing animals (Piet hated nature), fingers stiff from the cold, brain muddled by hunger, he could never get the dog right. Only the bright geometric pattern of the dog's sweater seemed to go well. Finally, in a fit of temporary madness, he hacked the canvas to pieces. When he came to his senses, minutes before the contest deadline, the only coherent chunk was the more or less finished sweater, which he submitted – and which (the club's membership being small) was good enough for the $10 third prize for best dog *accessory* painting. Piet immediately blew his prize money on a couple of T-bones and a bottle of claret, which he shared with an acquaintance named Babette, unaware that his deranged rendering of a dog sweater was destined to place him among the great names of the non-Objectivists.

The world has long debated the true meaning behind Edvard Munch's famous portrait of existential despair. This rare view of the original woodcut – as it existed before his agent advised him to add something, or eliminate something, but in any case, to do *something* to somehow make it seem more important – may, or may not, lay the matter to rest.

Rousseau painted from dreams
rather than life, and one of his recurring
night visions was of a gypsy sleeping
in the desert. Rousseau felt sure that the gypsy
was dreaming of him, and he longed to
wake him in order to confirm this. He first
sent a lion, but the lion only sniffed the sleeper.
He then sent (in a series of paintings that
have been lost or destroyed) a warthog, a dingo,
a giant anteater, a wombat, and an iguana.
All, like the lion, merely smelled the gypsy.
Interpreting all this as a message that scent was
an important element in this dream,
Rousseau painted the version shown: a standard
poodle carrying a fragrant rose, which did
in fact wake the gypsy. "Is your dream of me?"
Rousseau asked. "I don't know who you
may be," he answered, "but if it's any of your
business, I seem to have been dreaming
that I was at the zoo."

Claude Monet took huge pride in the gardens at his home in Giverny (he painted them dozens of times) and was just as hugely chagrined when he discovered his neighbor's dogs' penchants for digging in them. Repeated appeals to the lord of the adjacent manor availing nothing, Monet finally brought the matter to court. At this time, the use of the camera was common among the Impressionists, but it happened that, as an economy measure, Monet, Manet, Cezanne, Pisarro, and one or two others shared one – and it was currently Pisarro's turn. So Monet painted the scene he had so often witnessed – his neighbor's hounds laying waste to his garden – and unveiled the canvas in court.

The judge ruled that masterful brushwork and an uncannily accurate effect of softened evening light did not change the fact that a painting was a work of imagination and could not be accepted as evidence.

He found for the plaintiff.

More portraits were painted (61 are known) of George Washington than of any U.S. president since. One would wonder how he found the time for all those sittings if one were not aware of the role played by his bull terrier, Lafayette. The great man himself, it seems, allowed the painter fifteen minutes – from 6:00 to 6:15 A.M. – to rough in his shapes. From then on, he worked from Lafayette, who sat patiently for hours on end, even when fitted with an uncomfortable starched lace collar and a hot, musty, powdered wig. Remarkable as Lafayette's discipline and forebearance may have been, however, surely his resemblance to his master, sufficient as it was to serve as the model for more than sixty portraits, is more amazing. Yet, inexplicably, there is no record of anyone's making the slightest reference to it within the president's hearing.

Throughout his life, René Magritte carried on a copious correspondence with a wide circle of friends and colleagues. He often sent sketches of works in progress to other artists, including this one to Henri Matisse, which he wrote was "an exploration of certain dreamlike juxtapositions which ingeniously challenge the perception of reality versus image." Though the painting seems never to have been finished, the sketch came into the possession of Matisse's handyman, who was inspired by it to invent the Happi-Pup Weatherproof Dog Door, from which he became enormously wealthy. Magritte brought suit, on the grounds that he had originated the idea, but was denied in court. The judge pointed out that the drawing included, in Magritte's own handwriting, the words, *"Ceci n'est pas une porte de chien."* (This is not a dog door.)

An intense rivalry existed between Raphael and Michelangelo, and there was little they would stop at to gain a competitive edge. So Raphael was elated to overhear Pope Julius berating Michaelangelo concerning the work in the Sistine Chapel, though he could make out only intermittent snatches: "Complete lack of... dogs in the Vatican...correct this...immediately." Interpreting this as a criticism of his rival's work for its lack of dogs, Raphael rushed back to his own section of the chapel to paint the detail shown. Only later was he made aware that the pontiff was in fact instructing Michelangelo to remove his actual dog, Jupiter, from the Vatican grounds. Raphael rushed back to the chapel, intending to correct his error, but Pope Julius was already there. History does not record the ensuing conversation.

This image in cut paper and tempera has long puzzled art critics and historians because of its departure from Matisse's usual meticulously balanced compositions. The blank area in the lower right corner (see inset) has simply been unexplainable, until this letter from a glue manufacturer was found among Matisse's effects.

Dear M. Matisse:

Re your communication of the 23rd, we of course apologize for any embarrassment you have been caused. The particular batch of Mucilage Nonpareil from which you would have purchased your supply was indeed substandard, and has been recalled from the market. Please find enclosed our largest bottle of Mucilage Nonpareil, with our compliments. Mille pardons.

The owner of the Temple Fountain Diner, established in 1956 in Edward Hopper's home town of Providence, Rhode Island, was also the owner of some 27 dogs he had rescued from the city pound. Public health ordinances, of course, prohibited dogs inside the diner, but the eccentric proprietor never took this very seriously – especially after closing, when they were brought in to help clear the inventory of the day's unsold meatloaf specials. Though no health inspector was ever able to catch him at this, the restaurateur and canine benefactor was nevertheless forced to close the Temple Fountain in 1959, having bought, over the course of three years, at least eight times as much hamburger as he sold. This painting by Hopper was not publicly exhibited until 1974, when the last official of the county board of health during the Temple Fountain's heyday had retired or gone to his reward.

Throughout his life, Auguste Renoir's preferred subject matter was the social life of Paris's smart set. However, access to their balls, fetes, and soirees was not easy to come by for young and unestablished painters, so when a friend suggested he obtain a little dog as a sure means of gaining acceptance among even the most standoffish, he thought the idea ingenious. Unfortunately, he also thought that if a *little* dog was good, a *lot* of dog must be even better. For the next several years following *Breakup of the Boat Party*, Renoir's canvases continued to record the daily lives of sophisticated Parisians – as seen from a distance.

It has been suggested by more than one art critic that Modigliani's attenuated images may be the result of his being afflicted with acute astigmatic refraction, commonly known as El Greco Eyes. However, the common refutation of this theory has always been that Modigliani (unlike El Greco) lived in a time when such an impairment could easily have been corrected by eyeglasses. This recently discovered painting, entitled *"My Bloodhound Moriarty Chewing My Spectacles Again,"* perhaps reopens the controversy.

Degas, as much as he preferred to paint from real life, found the models too animated for concentrated studies and the camera too obtrusive for spontanaeity. His solution was his cousin's placid black Labrador, who was only too glad to sit for hours, begging for tidbits from the cafe patrons and barflies Degas wished to record. Yet later, when bragging to Monet, or possibly Manet, about his method of keeping the unaware model stationary, he was upbraided: "You have painted an absinthe drinker, *mon ami*, and you needed no subterfuge. You couldn't move an absinthe drinker with gunpowder. But you might have a painting here, if you delete the dog, and of course change the title." Which is how *The Biscuit Beggar* became *The Absinthe Drinker*.

When Henri de Toulouse-Lautrec haunted
the night spots of Paris, he brought, in
addition to his sketch pad and charcoal sticks, his
dog *Un Peu*, a high-spirited basset and
corgi mix. Since it was common for the cafes
and bistros to have resident cats, *Un Peu*
was often the source of no small disturbance.
After the dozenth time he had chased
Sabrina across the dance floor of the Moulin Rouge,
the proprietor insisted that *Un Peu* and Lautrec
must leave. Lautrec, always extremely sensitive
about the dwarfism that afflicted his legs,
said, "You are ejecting me because I am short,
n'est-ce pas?" "Not at all, m'sieur, it is because
of your damned dog. So far as I know,
your bill is paid in full. *Bon soir*."

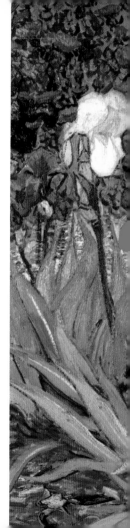

Having been allowed to paint his landlady's prized irises only on the condition that he would be financially responsible for any harm that might befall them, it is easy to imagine the pauper van Gogh's consternation at the discovery of this scene: the garden of Mme. Escallier (aka *La Scourge*) trampled and befouled by a homeless local dog with no bed of his own. Sympathetic as he was with any underdog, yet committed to artistic truth, van Gogh painted the scene exactly as he found it, knowing he would later feel the old lady's lash. Though his canvas did not minimize the damage, he did his best (knowing *La Scourge*'s nearsightedness) to give the poor dog a fighting chance at anonymity.

Degas loved to draw and paint the behind-the-scenes, sternly disciplined world of stage performers, especially ballet dancers. As he noted in his memoirs, "Their practice is so continuous, and so demanding, that they become as automatons. When the master shouts, 'Legs up to the bar!' all comply instantly, as if by unconscious instinct." Clearly the studio mascot, *Pas de Deux*, was not immune.

It is the rare artist who is commercially successful in his own lifetime, and more rare still is such overwhelming success as Gustav Klimt achieved with his most famous painting, *The Lovers*. It was bought for a huge sum on its first exhibition, and Klimt was soon besieged by other wealthy collectors to paint another – exactly like it – for them. In a public statement, he said, "Clearly, that would be wrong. A buyer of art has the right to expect his piece to be one of a kind – unique. I cannot paint another, for any price." In a more private moment, however, he asked, "Have you, by any chance, a dog? I could perhaps paint your dog, in…a certain setting." Eventually, he is known to have painted at least seventeen dogs in this way – no two alike.

To paint the Birth of Venus, Botticelli searched vainly for months for the perfect mortal model. His memoirs record that he finally compromised, taking some attributes from one, some from another. Though his principal model's name is lost to history, he wrote of her, "She has indeed the body of a goddess, but unfortunately the hair of a wharf rat. For the flowing tresses of my Venus, I must seek elsewhere, though I despair of finding such among all the women in Florence." Luckily, as this preliminary study shows, he extended his search among the women of Florence to include the dogs of Milan.

This painting, though similar
in most ways to many others by Haring
bears the distinction of his longest title:
A Man Will Pursue an Idiotic Goal
Until He Is Dead; a Dog Stops When He Is Tired.
Asked whether this bit of wisdom was
the result of his travels in the East,
he answered, "Exactly right: 44th and Bleeker.
East Village, Wing Fat's Chinese
and American Cuisine. Complimentary
fortune cookies for parties
of four or more."

It is not commonly known that, between his renunciation of commercial illustration and his establishment as America's icon of the avant-garde, Andy Warhol made a brief foray into the prosaic world of business, entering into a partnership with his uncle to launch Meaties, a new brand of dog food. The reasoning seemed to be that the uncle's long experience in the food service industry (he had managed a string of Stuckey's franchises in the Midwest) qualified him to head up production and sales, and Andy's experience on Madison Avenue meant that he could handle packaging and promotion, making Meaties Inc. a self-sufficient concern. However, when an art broker saw the Meaties label design and suggested that he could probably sell a lot of them *as paintings* (if some better-known consumer brand were represented), the lure of the bright track lighting of SoHo proved too much for Andy to resist.

Whether they depict soot-darkened city streets or storm-lashed Atlantic shores, Edward Hopper's paintings have become ultimate statements of loneliness and isolation. That is, they have become that to writers of art criticism; Hopper himself has consistently denied any such intention. At the exhibition of this, his last known painting, he was accosted by a particularly earnest member of the artistic press: "Does this not in fact sum up your entire body of work by observing the sameness of all environments, whether urban or 'natural,' as a result of humanity's appropriation of nature, the dog in this case symbolizing man's estrangement from his own uncivilized origins – his wild soul, if you will?" "No," Hopper replied. "It means leave me alone or I'll bite you really hard."

An interviewer once asked Picasso if he believed it was true that dogs and their owners come to resemble each other over time. His reply, *"El perro y el amo son de la misma pulga,"* may be loosely rendered in English as "As far as I'm concerned, they're pretty much the same to begin with."

In the later years of the nineteenth century, the glamour occupation of choice among Europeans was to be a painter, and any given afternoon saw the fields outside Paris bristling with portable easels and parasols. Not all of these practitioners were truly dedicated, of course, and they took to any means available to amuse themselves – which, out in the country, were not many – when the actual work began to pall. Flinging the lids of paint cans for their dogs to fetch was the one such activity that caught on, and it is still practiced by unemployed artists today.